CONTENTS

Some words are shown in **bold,** like this. You can find out what they mean by looking in the glossary.

DEATH IN THE DARK WOODS

Much of the landscape around us has changed through the centuries. People have created or altered farmland, parks, settlements, and roads. Other parts seem untouched by history. Mountains, grasslands, rivers, and forests look much as they did long ago. Yet these places – either wild or altered by humans – all have stories to tell. This book helps you discover these stories for yourself. It explains basic research techniques, and shows you where to find revealing **evidence**.

The vanishing legions

The Teutoburg Forest is located in a long range of wooded hills in northern Germany. Today, the area is a nature park, but it clearly has a shocking past because you may see place names such as "The Lane of Bones", "The Kettle of Slaughter", or "The Field of Victory". What could these names mean? And what bloody event took place here?

Over 2,000 years ago, the Roman Empire used its vast military power to conquer and control people in the region. In AD 9, three Roman **legions** marched into the Teutoburg Forest to put down an uprising and never came back. Over 20,000 soldiers, with their families, disappeared among the trees.

Many months later, the Romans learnt what had happened: a force of **Germanic** tribes had ambushed the three legions. Lost in the woods, terrified by storms, floundering on narrow muddy trails, they had been massacred. It was the greatest defeat ever suffered by the Roman Empire and is known as the Kalkriese massacre.

Amateur finds ammo   *i*

For many centuries, no one knew where the massacre had taken place. It was not until 1987 that a British amateur **archaeologist** began searching near a hill called Kalkriese. Tony Clunn, an off-duty soldier stationed in Germany, was amazingly lucky. Very soon, he found some Roman coins from the period of the battle. He later dug up several slingshot stones, a type of ammunition used in battle. This suggested for the first time that there had been fighting here.

Waltham Forest Libraries H

Please return this item by the last date stamped. The loan may be renewed unless required by another customer.

Jan 2015		

Need to renew your books?
http://www.londonlibraries.gov.uk/walthamforest or
Dial 0115 929 3388 for Callpoint – our 24/7 automated telephone renewal line. You will need your library card number and your PIN. If you do not know your PIN, contact your local library.

raintree

a Capstone company — publishers for children

Raintree is an imprint of Capstone Global Library Limited, a company incorporated in England and Wales having its registered office at 7 Pilgrim Street, London, EC4V 6LB Registered company number: 6695582

www.raintreepublishers.co.uk
myorders@raintreepublishers.co.uk

Text © Capstone Global Library Limited 2014
First published in hardback in 2014
First published in paperback in 2015
The moral rights of the proprietor have been asserted.

Edited by Andrew Farrow, James Benefield, and Adrian Vigliano
Designed by Tim Bond
Original illustrations © Capstone Global Library Ltd 2014
Picture research by Liz Alexander
Originated by Capstone Global Library Ltd
Production by Victoria Fitzgerald

Printed and bound in China

ISBN 978 1 406 27276 5 (hardback)
17 16 15 14 13
10 9 8 7 6 5 4 3 2 1

ISBN 978 1 406 27281 9 (paperback)
18 17 16 15 14
10 9 8 7 6 5 4 3 2 1

British Library in Cataloguing Publication Data
A full catalogue record for this book is available from the British Library.

Acknowledgements

We would like to thank the following for permission to reproduce photographs: Alamy pp. 5 (© Mark Harris), 15L (© The Protected Art Archive), 15r (© Richard Green), 17 (© A.P.S. (UK)), 23 (© James Steeves), 24 (© All Canada Photos), 53 (© Pictorial Press Ltd); Corbis pp. 7 (© Carmen Jaspersen/dpa), 18, 37 (© Szilard Koszticsak/epa), 48 (© JIM HOLLANDER/epa), 51 (© Elio Ciol); Getty Images pp. 9 (Robin Bush/Oxford Scientific), 10 (The British Library/ Robab via Getty Images), 12 (Peter Phipp/Photolibrary), 21 (Emory Kristof/National Geographic), 31 (AFP), 35 (Charley Yelen/Flickr), 55 (Xavier ROSSI/Gamma-Rapho via Getty Images), 57 (Design Pics/Guy Heitmann); Library of Congress p. 29; Mary Evans Picture Library p. 41 (Photograph by Frith & Co); Portable Antiquities Scheme/British Museum p. 6.; Shutterstock pp., 32 (© Andrey Burmakin), 39 (© Andrei Nekrassov), 45 (© SeanPavonePhoto), 46 (© WDF Photo); SuperStock pp. 27 (Aaron Huey/ National Geographic), 42 (Bridgeman Art Library, London).

Cover photograph: Main image: Sculpture entitled "Les Braves" by Anilore Banon on Omaha Beach in Normandy reproduced with permission from Shutterstock (© Bryan Busovicki); Inset left: D-DAY 1944 LCPV from USS Samuel Chase lands troops of US Army First Division reproduced from permission of Alamy (© Pictorial Press Ltd); Inset middle: American War Cemetery in Normany reproduced with permission from Shutterstock (© Alessandro Colle); Inset right: Gun emplacement at Omaha Beach reproduced with permission from Shutterstock (© Edward Haylan).

Disclaimer

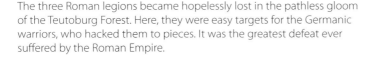

The three Roman legions became hopelessly lost in the pathless gloom of the Teutoburg Forest. Here, they were easy targets for the Germanic warriors, who hacked them to pieces. It was the greatest defeat ever suffered by the Roman Empire.

How do we know this story?

This disaster happened a long time ago. In that time, a lot of evidence has built up – most of it in recent years. Here are the key places where you would find this evidence if you were researching the story of the massacre today:

- The place itself: The site has specially laid out trails and an observation tower to help you understand the sequence of events. There is also plenty of deep forest to give you atmosphere.

- The objects found there: Many of these, such as a mask, slingshot, stones, and coins, are in the museum at the site.

- Ancient writings: Roman historians such as Tacitus and Suetonius recorded the event in books written about 100 years after the disaster had happened.

- Modern writings: Today's historians have used recent archaeological finds to give new accounts of the battle.

RESEARCH BASICS

How do you begin finding out about your subject? You may be researching a place for an individual school assignment or you may be doing it as part of a class project with other students. You may just want to know more about the background to your own garden or park. Whatever it is, you need to make connections between the piece of land you see today, and what happened there in the past.

Dave Crisp was an amateur archaeologist but he still found a hoard of Roman coins in Somerset in April 2010, using a metal detector. The product of this find became known as the Frome Hoard, and it comprised of over 50,000 coins.

Keep it simple. The huge choice of methods and sources for research can easily get confusing. Start by deciding what questions you want to ask about key themes and issues. Then look at the basic tools needed to answer them. Throughout this book, you will find guidance and ideas to help you.

Where should I look?

Where do you find your evidence? These are some of the most obvious starting points:

- The place itself: Of course, your basic source is the site. Use your eyes and ears to study it closely, and to listen to what local people (such as official guides) may have to say about it.

- The library: Libraries give you access to books, maps, DVDs, newspaper archives, and many other sources.

- The internet: A lot of source material is available online – if you know where to look. See page 43 for more advice on this.

- Museums: Specialist and local history museums contain a wealth of objects that can tell you a lot about an area and its development.

A regular festival commemorating the Kalkriese massacre is held in Kalkriese, in the Teutoburg Forest. Actors dressed in costume show how ancient soldiers fought. This is the product of much research, including the recovery of artefacts and sources.

Learning the language of research

Like most things, research has its own jargon (special language). Here are some of the basic terms you may come across.

The information you are looking for is called evidence. This is the raw material, made up of facts, figures, and other data, which provides a firm base for your project.

Evidence comes from two main sources. **Primary sources** are from the time of the events you are studying. They are usually created by people who were there and can describe the scene directly, and include diaries, letters, and photographs. Memories – oral or spoken – are also primary sources.

Artefacts are another vital primary source. These are the objects left behind or lost by previous cultures. They are often recovered by archaeologists who study the remains of the past.

Secondary sources are produced later. They are fresh accounts or interpretations of the events, by historians using primary or secondary source material. Secondary sources include history textbooks, biographies, encyclopaedias, and documentary films.

As the evidence piles up, you can easily be swamped by the material. To help, you can use graphic organizers. These are tools that help you shape your writing project, solve problems, plan research, and brainstorm ideas. There are many different kinds of organizers, including charts, webs, and tables.

Runnymede is a wide, flat, and low-lying piece of grassland on the bank of the River Thames just to the west of London. It is a water meadow, which means it probably flooded every winter when the Thames overflowed after heavy rain. This flooding left a deposit of rich **silt**, which made the land fertile and helped grass to grow well. In summer, the meadow was used to graze cattle and other livestock. It also has a momentous place in history.

The barons and the king

On 15 June 1215, there was a meeting at Runnymede. First to arrive were the **barons** and their fighting men. Then a much smaller group approached. This was King John, England's ruler, with his court officials and religious leaders. The Archbishop of Canterbury read out a long document, and the king set his royal seal on it, to show that he approved. Mounting his horse again, the king rode back to his castle at Windsor. The document was to be called Magna Carta, which is Latin for "The Great Charter".

The name of the field where John and the nobles met comes from two Anglo-Saxon words put together. It comes from *run* meaning council, and *mede* meaning field or meadow. Together, they mean "meadow where regular meetings are held". Runnymede had probably been a gathering place for many years before 1215. In fact, the Anglo-Saxon King Alfred had held open-air meetings with his Witan (Council) here during the 9th century AD. However, the sealing of Magna Carta was the most influential event in Runnymede's history.

Zoom in: The Ankerwycke Yew

Amazingly, there may be one witness to the Magna Carta agreement still alive today. It is a tree – the Ankerwycke Yew, which is calculated to be nearly 2,000 years old. The yew stands on the riverbank opposite Runnymede, and it was first mentioned in the 1085 Domesday Book (a record of all property in England, made by the Normans). The tree was there at the time of King John, and was the spot where a later king, Henry VIII, met his second wife, Anne Boleyn, in 1526.

The Ankerwycke Yew, located near Runnymede, is one of the oldest trees in the UK. It has been there for nearly 2,000 years, when the country was ruled by the Romans.

Rebels against the king

Why did this great meeting take place? This was the climax of a long period of revolt. The barons were the most powerful and wealthy men in England, whose families had sworn to serve and obey the monarch. But many of them were angry with King John, whom they saw as a failure and a bully. He had lost some of his territory in France, quarrelled with the Pope, and also increased taxation.

Several barons began an open rebellion against the king in May 1215. They drew up a programme (or charter) of government reforms. When King John refused to agree to it, the rebels attacked and took control of London, his capital city. Now there was really no choice. King John was forced to meet the barons at Runnymede and give in to their demands. This incident would have a lasting impact on British history.

The Great Charter

What was the document sealed by the king on Runnymede? It was made of **parchment**. The words on it were written by **scribes** (who were probably monks) using ink and quill pens. The king did not "sign" the document. Instead, he pressed his royal seal into hot wax at the bottom of the parchment to indicate it had his approval.

The document that became known as the Magna Carta contained a list of 63 clauses. Some of these recognized the privileges of the church and of the barons and other noblemen. For instance, the king could not raise new taxes unless the nobles and church leaders agreed. Other clauses dealt with the justice system and with people's rights and freedoms.

> ### *Freedom and justice*   *i*
> "No free man shall be seized or imprisoned, or stripped of his rights or possessions, or outlawed or exiled. Nor will we proceed with force against him, except by the lawful judgement of his equals or by the law of the land. To no one will we sell, to no one deny or delay right or justice."
>
> *Magna Carta, 1215, clauses 39 and 40 (translated from the original Latin)*

Time has taken its toll on the condition of the Magna Carta, signed back in the 13th century. Now, only four copies of the original Magna Carta still survive.

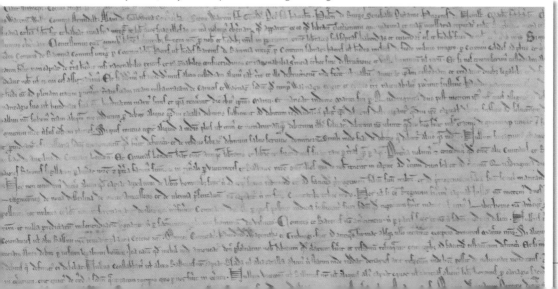

A statement of rights

At first, Magna Carta had a very limited impact. It was mainly created to help the barons and other powerful people by asserting their traditional rights and curbing the powers of the king. Only much later, in the 17th century, did people recognize the Charter as a statement of the legal rights of everyone – rich and poor alike. It became one of the most famous documents in the world. Why is it so important? There are two main reasons:

- This was the first time an English monarch had officially agreed to limit his or her royal **authority**. It made clear that the law was a form of power in its own right. The king was subject to the law, and not above it.

- The most famous clause in the charter established that no free person could be put in prison, or have their possessions taken away, or be **outlawed** or sent into **exile** unless he or she had a fair and lawful trial by other free citizens (see the box "Freedom and justice"). This gave a legal basis to every individual's right to liberty and justice, which has since been echoed in many other countries around the world.

Magna Carta today

However, in Britain, only three of the original 63 clauses in the Charter are still part of the law. The first one protects the freedoms of the Church. The second deals with the independent powers of London and other large towns. The third (which is detailed above) establishes the right of free people to a just legal trial when accused of a crime. The document's power, though, remains undiminished.

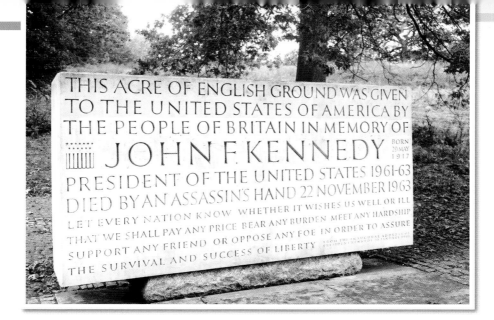

THIS ACRE OF ENGLISH GROUND WAS GIVEN
TO THE UNITED STATES OF AMERICA BY
THE PEOPLE OF BRITAIN IN MEMORY OF
JOHN F. KENNEDY BORN 29 MAY 1917
PRESIDENT OF THE UNITED STATES 1961-63
DIED BY AN ASSASSIN'S HAND 22 NOVEMBER 1963
LET EVERY NATION KNOW WHETHER IT WISHES US WELL OR ILL
THAT WE SHALL PAY ANY PRICE BEAR ANY BURDEN MEET ANY HARDSHIP
SUPPORT ANY FRIEND OR OPPOSE ANY FOE IN ORDER TO ASSURE
THE SURVIVAL AND SUCCESS OF LIBERTY FROM THE INAUGURAL ADDRESS OF PRESIDENT KENNEDY IN JANUARY 1961

After US President John F. Kennedy was assassinated in 1963, an acre of
Runnymede was given to the United States in his memory. Here, a stone pathway
has been built, leading to a stone slab inscribed with words by President Kennedy.

Runnymede remembrance

Several memorials have been built at Runnymede, in honour of the place's
role in the development of just government. The Commonwealth Air Forces
Memorial is a massive structure commemorating the 20,000 men and
women of the **Allied** air forces who died in World War II, and whose bodies
were never found.

The Magna Carta Memorial was erected in 1957. It was paid for by the
American Bar Association, a group of US lawyers. Magna Carta is very
significant to Americans because it was used in 1776 to justify their rebellion
against British rule.

Magna Carta mystery

At least one big question about Magna Carta has never been answered:
where exactly did King John meet the barons? Nobody knows for certain. The
only evidence comes from the document itself, which gives the location as
"the meadow that is called Runnymede, between Windsor and Staines".

However, this may refer not just to the meadow, but also to the whole area
on either side of the Thames. Just across the river from the meadow is an
island – now called Magna Carta Island. Many people believe this is where the
Charter was read and sealed.

Where should I look?

Here are some suggestions for beginning research on Runnymede and Magna Carta:

- Go to the site itself: Runnymede is a major tourist attraction, and is run by the National Trust. Visiting here might help you picture the signing of the Magna Carta, and you can visit the Magna Carta Memorial. It is open during the day throughout most of the year. See the website at **www.nationaltrust.org.uk/runnymede**

- See the original Magna Carta: The first version, sealed by the king, has been lost. But four copies, made in 1215, have survived. Two of them are in the British Library in London, and the others are in Lincoln Cathedral, Lincolnshire and Salisbury Cathedral, Wiltshire.

- Read it online: On the British Library website (**www.bl.uk/treasures/magnacarta/translation/mc_trans.html**), you can examine the original text and read a full translation in English.

Making a connection: The legacy of Runnymede

Magna Carta is regarded as a key document in world history. How can you make connections between this ancient Latin text and the ideals of many modern governments? Here are some ideas to help you:

- Magna Carta had a significant influence on the founders of the American nation, as the US **Constitution** of 1787 shows. Compare the sections on freedom with liberty under the law in both of these important documents.

- Many of today's laws in the United Kingdom, the United States, and other countries are based on the Charter's principles. For an example of this, find out about the law of Habeas Corpus (see the website **http://magnacarta800th.com/history-of-the-magna-carta/the-magna-carta-timeline/1679-the-habeas-corpus-act**).

- Make a list of the major rights and freedoms declared in Magna Carta. Do you live in a country where these are upheld by the government? If you do, imagine what it would be like if these rights did not exist.

YOUR COMMUNITY

Leslie Hurst was born and raised in the village of Maywood, Illinois, USA. After finishing school in 1962, he moved away and rarely returned. Nearly half a century later, he was sent the link to a website exploring Maywood's past. This inspired him to record his own memories of the place and post them online. His article revealed a fact few people knew: the Hursts had been the first black family ever to settle in Maywood. Today, the community regularly celebrates its long history of diversity.

A unique story

A community is a group of people. It is also a geographical place – largely created by those people. Each community has its own special character, which makes it different from other communities. This means that every community has a unique history. With luck, some of this unique character will have survived over the years.

How much do you know about your local community? On the surface, it may not seem to have a very rich or interesting past. It may be a modern settlement, with brand new buildings and facilities, or a neighbourhood that has been swallowed up by noisy roads and giant office blocks. But once you begin digging into the history of the area, you could be in for a surprise.

Questions to ask

The first and most vital question to ask is: why was this place chosen for a settlement? The answer will probably be connected to its geography. Many communities grow up in places that have a geographical importance, such as:

- River crossings: Rivers were an obstacle to travellers, so roads naturally headed for fords, bridges, and other crossing points. Communities developed at these places.

- Crossroads: Trading routes became major roads. Places where these roads crossed were ideal for markets, shops, and other commerce, so settlements sprang up there.

In a community, the use of a place can change over time. These photographs show the same place in New York City. In the 1890s (left), this place was a busy thoroughfare, with carts and trams. On the right is same place in the modern day. There is still some traffic, but some of the street is now used for places to eat, drink, and socialize.

- Harbours: Some parts of the coast have natural harbours, which often grew into major ports for fishing and cargo ships.

- Natural resources: Wherever natural resources such as coal or iron are plentiful, communities have usually grown up near by.

Other questions include: When was the community first established? What was there before? What are the main physical features (such as a river, or a crossroads) that influenced its development? From here, you can go into greater detail.

Zoom in: Ford of the oxen

Oxford is one of the most famous university towns in the world. But why did it grow up where it did? The main clue is in the name: the word "ford" tells us that it began as a shallow place on a river where people and animals could cross easily. In fact, Oxford's name comes from two Anglo-Saxon words: *oxena* and *forde,* meaning "place where the oxen [cattle] cross". A settlement started growing during, and shortly after, the reign of King Alfred in the late 9th century. It is now a small city!

The roots of research

When doing research, answers will mostly be found by examining documents, studying land and buildings, and talking to people.

1) Looking at documents

Here are some places to look for documents locally:

- Libraries often have a local history section.

- Museums contain varied and often surprising material.

- Newspaper offices may let you use their libraries of cuttings (interesting extracts) and view old newspapers (known as back numbers).

- Local archives and county record offices contain a wealth of vital material, including **census** records, registers of electors, parish registers, and family papers.

Other documents are in national sources, which you can access online:

- The Land Registry is the official keeper of land ownership details in England and Wales. Its site is **www.landregistry.gov.uk**. For information in Scotland, use **www.scotlandlandregistry.co.uk**. In Northern Ireland, use **www.dfpni.gov.uk/lps/index/land_registration-2/the_land_registry.htm**

- The National Archives is the government's official archive, containing a huge variety of data. It can be found at this site: **www.nationalarchives.gov.uk**

2) Looking at land and buildings

The most accessible primary source is the neighbourhood itself. You can find out a lot by studying what you can see on the ground. This includes:

- Buildings: How old are the houses, churches, and other structures? What did the factories manufacture?

- Roads: The routes taken by old roads, streets, and footpaths often remain unchanged for centuries. Who originally used them?

- Watercourses: Settlements often grew up at places where a river was easy to cross. Rivers were also important transport routes.

- Railways: Most railways were built during the 19th century. How did they change the landscape?

- Cemeteries: Gravestone inscriptions give clues to the past.

Looking at your surroundings can bring up all kinds of interesting facts. This aerial view of an English town shows a mixture of the old (the long high street, the cathedral) and the new (new houses).

3) Talking to people

Local people can know a lot about the community. By talking to them, you may be able to get information that you could not find elsewhere. Act sensitively, explain exactly what your project is, and have a list of questions. However, remember that some stories may be based in myth, not fact!

The most important contact may be with local history groups. The members may already have done a large amount of neighbourhood research, and may even have written books about it. For contacts, ask at your library. The group might also help you find other people to talk to, such as long-term residents.

> ### *What does that name mean?* *i*
> Names can tell you a lot. First, look at the name of the community, which will give a big clue about its origins. Street names all have meanings, too. Some, such as "Main Street" or "High Street", are obvious, but other meanings may have been changed or been forgotten over time. For instance, a street called "The Shambles" was originally full of butchers' shops (the word comes from the Anglo-Saxon word *sceamol*, meaning "place where meat is butchered").

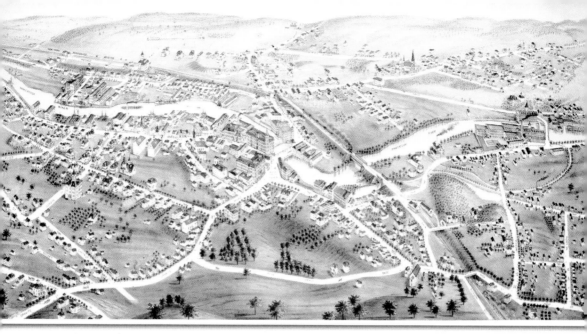

Many early maps were pictures from a bird's eye view rather than the accurate plans we see today. This one, of Westerly, Rhode Island, USA, in 1877, shows buildings and other features in three dimensions.

Local history from maps

Studying maps of an area over different periods can show vital details of how it has changed and grown. Maps give hard evidence of how boundary lines, paths, roads, and waterways have gradually altered through the centuries. Maps also demonstrate the effects of bigger and faster developments, such as the building of factories and housing estates, and the construction of railways and motorways.

You can find many kinds of maps in libraries and record offices:

- Old maps: Before about 1750, maps were not very accurately drawn. However, many showed buildings in elevation (as seen from the ground), which can make at least the buildings easier to identify.

- Ordnance Survey (OS) : This survey mapped Britain accurately for the first time by the early 1800s. OS maps have been updated ever since, and give a wonderful overview of the changing towns and countryside. Many OS maps (even early ones) are available online at this website:
  www.magazine.ordnancesurveyleisure.co.uk/magazine/tscontent/ editorials/getamap/os-getamap-home.html

- **Tithe** maps: These are accurate, large-scale maps of every parish in England, drawn up in the late 1830s. You can see them at your local records office, although some are also available through the National Archives.

Make a timeline

i

One of the simplest sorts of graphic organizer is a timeline. This is a list of important dates set out in chronological (time) order. It gives a framework to your research project, and is especially useful for a subject with a long and varied history, such as a community. Here is how you might begin a timeline (the place is not a real one):

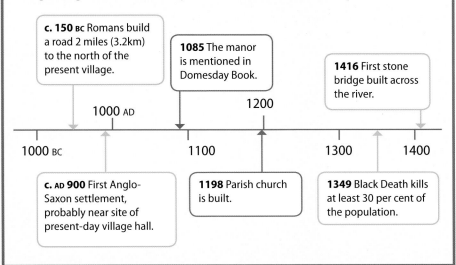

c. 150 BC Romans build a road 2 miles (3.2km) to the north of the present village.

1085 The manor is mentioned in Domesday Book.

1416 First stone bridge built across the river.

1000 AD

1200

1000 BC   1100   1300   1400

c. AD 900 First Anglo-Saxon settlement, probably near site of present-day village hall.

1198 Parish church is built.

1349 Black Death kills at least 30 per cent of the population.

Research roadshow: Summit County veterans

"This is the most forgotten war," says Sharon Myers. "Nobody seems to know anything about it." She is talking about the War of 1812 fought between the United States and Britain over control of the Great Lakes. Sharon is president of a local history group in Summit County, Ohio, USA, dedicated to reviving the memory of how the conflict affected their community. For example, how many soldiers came from the area? Using history books, military rosters, and cemetery records, the group came up with a detailed list of 350 names, ranks, and dates. Then they started on the painstaking process of finding and photographing every single grave (many were not even marked). The result was a priceless record of lots of veterans who might have otherwise disappeared from the public's memory.

VIKINGS AND VINLAND

Usually, we look at a place to tell us about history. However, sometimes we know the history first, but the place where it happened is a mystery. In this chapter, we look at the first Europeans to reach America.

The voyage of Leif Ericsson

For many years, people generally believed that a boatload of Norse (Scandinavian) people landed on the north-east coast of North America in the year 1001 – five centuries before Christopher Columbus (1451–1506) crossed the Atlantic. The only evidence for this was the story told in two Norse **sagas**, written down about two centuries later. These told how 35 sailors, led by Leif Ericsson, set sail from Greenland in search of a great land they had heard stories about.

The expedition reached this unknown land, then explored southwards down the coast. Eventually, they discovered a region with lush fields, fresh water, and plenty of fish and game to eat. Leif called this Vinland. The party spent the winter there, then returned to Greenland, full of praise for this new country. The sagas tell of later voyages to Vinland, and the building of a settlement. But then the Norsemen had a violent encounter with a local people they called the skraelings (probably Native American people). After this, they abandoned the settlement.

Zoom in: The Norse sagas

The sagas are a primary source for research into Viking settlements. They are medieval stories about the ancient Norsemen, or Vikings, around the year AD 1000. The sagas told of their voyages to Iceland, Greenland, and North America, of their kings, family histories, and bloody conflicts. Starting out as oral (spoken) stories, they were eventually written down in the Old Norse language in about 1250, many years after the events happened. The two which contain the story of Vinland are called *The Saga of Erik the Red* and *The Saga of the Greenlanders*.

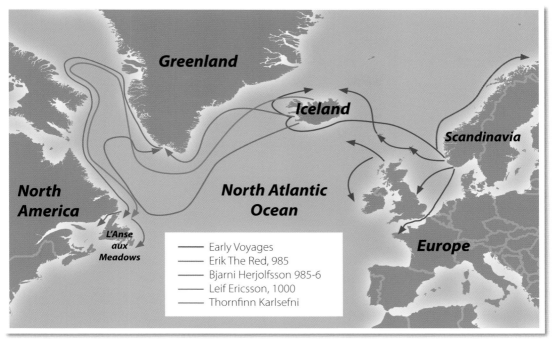

This map shows significant Norse journeys, including those of Leif Ericsson. This map is based on several historical maps, which were are far less accurate than most maps today.

The search for Vinland

What proof was there that this had actually happened? No definite evidence of the Norse settlement was found until 1960. Norwegian explorer Helge Ingstad and his wife Anne, an archaeologist, had made a close study of the saga. They explored much of New England and Nova Scotia on foot, searching for the place where Leif had landed.

At last, the Ingstads reached a point on the north coast of Newfoundland, Canada. Helge asked a local fisherman if he knew of any ancient ruins nearby. The man led them "to a beautiful place with lots of grass and a small creek and some mounds in the tall grass. It was very clear that this was a very, very old site."

Archaeologists uncovered hearths made of flat stones in the houses at L'Anse aux Meadows.

Digging at Jellyfish Bay

The site found by the Ingstads was called L'Anse aux Meadows. Its name has nothing to do with meadows, but comes from the French words *meduse* meaning "jellyfish" and *anse* meaning "bay". It is on the coast of the northern tip of the island of Newfoundland.

In the 1960s and 1970s, the Ingstads and archaeologists from North American park services dug up the area. Beneath overgrown mounds, they uncovered parts of eight houses. The walls and roofs had been made of earth and **peat** slabs placed over a framework of timber. Later, they also found the remains of a forge for making and working iron, and four workshops.

The Vikings were here

Somebody had definitely lived at L' Anse aux Meadows long ago. The evidence at the site showed that these settlers had been Norse people. The proof came from such things as:

• Walls and roofs: The buildings had been constructed in the same way as houses in Norway and Greenland during the same period, with peat walls, steep pointed roofs, and earth floors.

• Fires: The main houses each had a fire-pit in the middle, with earth benches round them. Another hut had a simple sauna (steam bath), paved with pebbles. These would have been heated with fire and then sprinkled with water to produce steam for bathing. Both of these features were typical of Scandinavian houses at the time.

• Artefacts: The teams also found a number of artefacts that were almost certainly made by Viking craftsmen, including a stone oil lamp, part of a spindle (for spinning wool), a bone needle, and a bronze pin (which Vikings used for fastening their cloaks).

Where and what was Vinland?   *i*

L'Anse aux Meadows is a Viking site. However, no one can definitely prove it was part of Leif's Vinland. There are still many mysteries to solve about Vinland – not only its location but also its name. See what you can find out. A good place to start is **www.canadianmysteries.ca/sites/ vinland/home/indexen.html**

This is a reconstruction of a Viking house. On the left and on the right, you can see the wooden posts that held up the steep pointed roof. You can also see the position of the fire-pit in the middle of the floor. Vikings didn't have to worry about the fire damaging any carpets, rugs, or floorboards with their earth floor!

Zoom in: Leif Ericsson's ship

Everyone knows what a Viking warship (or longship) looked like – long and narrow. But Leif used a different kind of vessel, better suited to long voyages and rough seas. This was called a knarr, and was broader, with room for cargo and provisions. It was built of oak and pine, with a big cloth sail. There is a model of a knarr in Denmark's Roskilde Viking Ship Museum (see **www.vikingeskibsmuseet.dk/en**).

Who else lived at L'Anse aux Meadows?

Long before the Vikings arrived, there were communities on this site. The earliest settlers lived here in about 4000 BC. They were probably attracted by food and other resources. There was a rich supply of fish, seal meat, and other seafood, and wild game in the woodlands (which covered much of the area at that time).

The excavations at L'Anse aux Meadows showed that there had been at least five other sets of residents at this place. Archaeologists found fragments of tools and traces of fire hearths. The last of these very early settlers were Inuit (or Eskimo) peoples who lived by this shore until about two centuries before Leif landed.

Part of the settlement at L'Anse aux Meadows has been reconstructed. The large building in this photograph is the longhouse, where the settlers lived. The other buildings you can see in this picture are workshops or storehouses. The buildings and grazing land for livestock are surrounded by a fence, to protect them.

Why is this place so important?

The discovery and excavation of L'Anse aux Meadows was a milestone in the history of human exploration. It is the earliest evidence of a European settlement on the American continent. It is also the first and only site definitely known to have been established by the Vikings in North America.

Today, the settlement is officially a National Historic Site of Canada, and a UNESCO World Heritage Site. Visitors can see reconstructions of three Norse buildings, view exhibitions about Viking life and history, and walk trails to the surrounding bays and lakes. You can find out more on the official Parks Canada website: **www.pc.gc.ca/eng/lhn-nhs/nl/meadows/visit.aspx**

Research roadshow:
Where else did the Vikings go?

The great age of the Vikings lasted from about AD 800 to 1050. During that time, Norse merchants, pirates, and explorers sailed over a vast area, and built settlements in Europe (including modern Russia), North Africa, and Asia, as well as North America. Here are just a few Viking sites discovered by archaeologists that also have stories to tell:

- York: York (or Jorvik) was an important Viking settlement. Excavations in the 1980s uncovered much vital evidence of trade and daily life. The site now houses a major Viking exhibition (see **jorvik-viking-centre. co.uk/about-jorvik**).

- Thingvellir, Iceland: The Icelandic Vikings held their national parliamentary meetings in this dramatic open-air setting. It is now part of a national park.

- Brattahlid, Greenland: The Vikings built the first ever church in Greenland. A modern replica now stands in its place.

- Dublin, Ireland: Builders preparing ground for a block of flats in central Dublin in the 1970s discovered remains of a huge Viking settlement. Artefacts from here are on display at the National Museum of Ireland and at Dublinia (**www.dublinia.ie**).

WOUNDED KNEE

Wounded Knee Creek flows through the Pine Ridge **Reservation** in South Dakota, USA. This has been a sacred spot for American Indians for many years. According to legend, the body of the great Sioux warrior Crazy Horse was buried here after being killed by US troops in 1877. No one has ever found his resting place. But Wounded Knee Creek has another, even more tragic, meaning for American Indian people. It was the setting for the incident that ended a long, bitter chapter in US history – the **Plains Indian** Wars.

The destruction of the Sioux

The Sioux were the biggest group among the Plains Indians. They were also the most successful opponents of the invasion by white settlers. Their greatest act of resistance came in June 1876, in the Black Hills of Dakota. Led by chiefs including Crazy Horse, they wiped out a **cavalry** unit led by General George Custer at the Battle of the Little Bighorn.

The US government took immediate revenge. During 1877, the US Army swept across the Plains, destroying American Indian villages and forcing the Sioux and other natives onto reservations far from their homes. The Sioux nation was confined to poor-quality land inside present-day North and South Dakota, a few kilometres from Wounded Knee Creek. Unable to hunt for their food, they depended on handouts from the government, and many died from disease.

Zoom in: The Plains Indian Wars

In the early 1800s, the white population of America was expanding westward, onto land where American Indians had lived for centuries. In 1830, a new law forced these American Indians even further west, into the vast empty spaces of the Great Plains. By the 1850s, white immigrants were flooding across the Plains as well. There were violent confrontations between natives and settlers, which became a very one-sided war in 1864. American Indians won a few small victories, but had no real chance against the bigger and better-armed forces of the white US government. When the war ended in 1890, the native people had lost their lands and way of life forever.

In 1903, survivors of the massacre and relatives of the victims erected a memorial at Wounded Knee Creek. The memorial lists all those who had been killed. There is a visitor centre nearby, which gives visitors more information about the massacre and a history of American Indians.

Spotted Elk's last journey

On 15 December 1890, government police shot dead the most famous of all Sioux chiefs, Sitting Bull. His remaining followers were terrified by the violence. A group of Sioux men, women, and children escaped from the reservation and fled southwards, hoping to find refuge. Their leader was an old and ill chief called Spotted Elk.

The US Government immediately issued a warrant for the arrest of Spotted Elk (whom they called Big Foot). On 28 December, troops of the US 7th Cavalry caught up with him and his band of cold and hungry refugees. The chief himself was coughing up blood, and was so ill that he was being carried in a wagon. When he saw the troops, he had a white flag of surrender raised.

The cavalry commander, James Forsyth, had orders to take the band to the nearest railway, so they could be sent on to prison. But it was already late afternoon, so he decided to camp near by. The Sioux were escorted down into the valley, next to the frozen Wounded Knee Creek.

Preparing for action

In the bitter cold, the Sioux erected their tipis (a form of tent) next to the dry **ravine** that led down to the creek. Spotted Elk was given medical treatment, and a stove was placed in his tent to warm him.

A force of 470 well-armed soldiers guarded the 350 Sioux, but James Forsyth was taking no chances. He still believed his captives might be dangerous, so he ordered four Hotchkiss guns to be set up on the hill above the camp. These weapons could fire over 40 explosive shells per minute.

Massacre

The next morning, 29 December, Forsyth stationed a long line of armed soldiers south of the ravine. More stood in a curve to the north of the Indian camp. Behind them, on the hill, four teams of gunners waited behind their Hotchkiss guns.

Forsyth told the Sioux they had to give up all of their weapons. Soldiers moved into the tipis to search for anything hidden. The Sioux were scared and angry. There was an argument, and a shot rang out. Immediately, the soldiers opened fire with their rifles. Then the Hotchkiss guns poured shells into the camp.

Where should I look?

There is a vast amount more to find out about the Plains Indian Wars. Start off by looking at the following websites:

www.indians.org/articles/american-indians.html

www.pbs.org/wgbh/amex/weshallremain

If you would like to read very detailed accounts of the events, the following two books are ideal:

Bury My Heart at Wounded Knee: An Indian History of the American West, Dee Brown (Sterling Publications, 2009)

The West: An Illustrated History, Geoffrey C. Ward (Weidenfeld & Nicolson, 1996)

The dead bodies were left on the ground for three days, frozen in a blizzard. Then they were buried in a mass grave on top of the hill. This was also where the Hotchkiss guns had been positioned during the slaughter.

Buried at Wounded Knee

The slaughter lasted for only a few minutes. When it ended, over 200 Sioux lay dead, including Spotted Elk himself, and many others were fatally wounded. About 25 soldiers had also been killed, most by stray shots from their own side. That night, a blizzard of snow covered the area, so the Sioux corpses could not be recovered until three days later. They were buried in a mass grave on the hill above the creek.

This one-sided fight marked the end of the 36-year war. The much stronger forces of the US Army had finally crushed the American Indians who lived on the Great Plains. The survivors of the Sioux and other native nations had lost their independence and their lands forever. Wounded Knee Creek became a **symbol** of government savagery.

> ### *Eyewitness: A survivor of the massacre*
> "I was badly wounded and pretty weak, too. I looked down the ravine and saw a lot of women coming and crying. I saw soldiers on both sides of the ravine shoot at them until they had killed every one of them. One woman was crying 'Mother! Mother!'"
>
> *Dewey Beard (1858–1955), a Sioux warrior who survived the massacre*

Recording the truth

Most white people in the United States were relieved that the threat of the Indian Wars had ended. But others wanted the bloody massacre of Spotted Elk's band to be remembered by future generations. Soon afterwards, those who had lived through it formed the Wounded Knee Survivors Association.

At first, the members just wanted to get **compensation** from the government for their suffering. In 1903, they erected a memorial on the battlefield, listing all those who had died. Part of the inscription reads: "Many innocent women and children who knew no wrong died here." By the 1970s, the Association's aims were to preserve the site at Wounded Knee Creek and protect it from exploitation by farmers or builders.

Making a connection: What other atrocities were committed at this time?

White Europeans came to North America in search of land and wealth. They used their force of numbers and superior weapons to clear American Indians out of their way. However, they were not the only invaders to commit **atrocities** against indigenous people in this period. Other examples include:

- 1864–1870: The Russian Tsar (Emperor) expelled the Circassian people from the Northwest Caucasus. Hundreds of thousands were forced out of their homeland. A vast (and unknown) number died of disease, shipwreck, starvation, and Russian-inflicted violence.

- 1885–1908: King Leopold of Belgium took control of Congo. The Belgians treated the inhabitants as slave labour and exploited valuable natural resources, including rubber and minerals. Some historians believe over 10 million Congolese died in this period.

- 1937: Japanese forces invaded China and captured the city of Nanking. During the bloodshed that followed, the invaders murdered at least 250,000 people, often in brutal ways. The appalling slaughter by the Japanese lasted for eight weeks, leaving the city half destroyed and littered with corpses.

The Wounded Knee Incident

On 27 February 1973, the name of Wounded Knee rang round the world once again. A group of around 200 people, including Sioux and other protestors, **occupied** the small town of Wounded Knee (near the creek). They were angry at official corruption, and at the US government's failure to keep its promises to American Indians. They chose the town because of its symbolic importance to the Sioux. The protests lasted for 71 days before police regained control.

Sioux protestors occupied the town of Wounded Knee in 1973. They protested over the failure of the US Government's Bureau of Indian Affairs (BIA) to promote the rights of American Indian people.

Wounded Knee today

The US government classified the site as a National Historic Landmark in 1965, which means it is a place of huge significance to the whole country. But what can you see there today? There are still a few buildings dotting the landscape, including the original memorial, a timber church, and a museum and visitor centre.

Every year since 1986, the massacre has been commemorated by the Big Foot Memorial Ride (after the soldiers' name for Spotted Elk). This is a horseback journey of 307 kilometres (191 miles) in midwinter through South Dakota, which ends at Wounded Knee Creek. The riders carry a white flag as a symbol of their hopes for world peace. At the site, they say prayers to remember the victims.

American Maury Kravitz was a very rich man, but he still had one big ambition. He thought he knew the location in Mongolia of the lost tomb of Genghis Khan. In 2002, Kravitz used his wealth to take a team of archaeologists there. However, workers were bitten by snakes, and vital equipment was lost. Finally, the team was accused of damaging a sacred site and ordered out of the country. They never found the tomb.

Where is Genghis Khan buried?

A modern statue of Genghis Khan stands in Mongolia's capital, Ulan Bator.

This chapter is about a specific place that has links with history – but somewhere that is still unknown. It is a long detective story that has not yet reached a conclusion. When the great Genghis Khan died in China in August 1227, his body was placed on a wagon and carried back to the region of his birth. This was the Mongolian **steppes**, an area of windswept grassland, bare hills, and mountains. Any person or animal who witnessed this procession was killed.

Somewhere in eastern Mongolia, the procession halted. A vast grave was dug, and Genghis Khan's coffin was placed in it, covered by a huge felt *yurt* (circular tent used by **nomadic** Mongolians), and surrounded with jewels, weapons, food, and drink. They filled the hole with soil, and soldiers guarded the site to prevent anyone from coming near. Moss, grass, and trees grew over the grave. No one has ever succeeded in finding it again.

The long search

In the nearly 800 years since Genghis Khan's death, many people have looked for his tomb. Many, like Kravitz, believed they had found vital clues that would lead them there. However, so far all of them have been proved wrong. How can you research something if you do not know where it is?

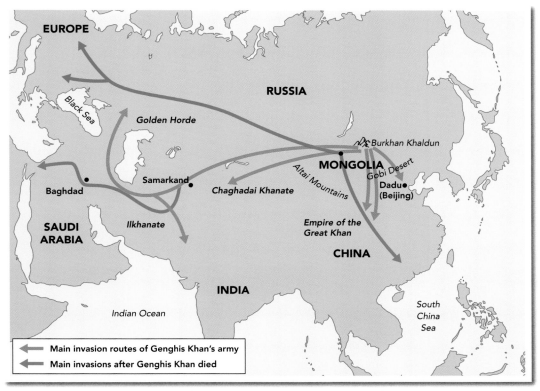

EUROPE

RUSSIA

Black Sea

Golden Horde

Burkhan Khaldun

MONGOLIA

Altai Mountains

Gobi Desert

Samarkand

Baghdad

Chaghadai Khanate

Dadu
(Beijing)

SAUDI
ARABIA

Ilkhanate

Empire of the
Great Khan

CHINA

INDIA

Indian Ocean

South
China
Sea

◄— Main invasion routes of Genghis Khan's army

◄— Main invasions after Genghis Khan died

This map shows the areas invaded by Genghis Khan and his armies. It also
shows the later Mongol invasions. After Genghis Khan died, Mongol territory
grew into the largest contiguous empire (containing countries with common
borders) ever created.

Zoom in: The world conqueror

Temujin (Genghis Khan's real name) was born in about 1162 into
the nomadic tribes of the steppe. His bravery and cunning soon gained
him followers, and by 1206, the Mongols had proclaimed him "Genghis
Khan", or "Ruler of the World". He led his fearsome army of horsemen to
conquer northern China, Central Asia, Afghanistan, and much of Persia.
This created the biggest empire the world had yet seen, stretching
from the Black Sea to the South China Sea. Temujin was also an efficient
ruler, who gave the Mongols a code of law and an alphabet.

What clues are there?

Because the tomb was unmarked, there are no physical signs on the ground to show us where it was. The only clues we have come from ancient writings, and from the beliefs of the modern Mongolian people. These clues point to the eastern part of Mongolia, and the province of Khentii, on the border with Russia. Here stands the mountain called Burkhan Khaldun. Why should we believe the tomb is here?

- It is Temujin's birthplace: The oldest of all Mongolian texts, *The Secret History of the Mongols*, was probably written a few years after Genghis Khan's death. It states that his ancestors lived at Burkhan Khaldun. Mongol chiefs were usually buried near their birthplace.

- Temujin took refuge there from his enemies: The mountain was special to him for another reason. When he was still a young man, a strong band of enemies raided his camp and kidnapped his wife. Outnumbered, Temujin ran away and hid on the wooded slopes of Burkhan Khaldun (he later took revenge and rescued his wife).

- It is in the Forbidden Zone: After Temujin's death, the area around Burkhan Khaldun was named Ikh Khorig. This means the "Great **Taboo**" or the "Forbidden Zone". The land was guarded by a group of 50 armed families, who had orders to kill any trespassers. The ban remained in force until 1989, when the first visitors and archaeological expeditions were allowed in. Why do you think Ikh Khorig remained off limits for so long?

Genghis Khan's vow *i*

The Secret History of the Mongols is the oldest surviving Mongolian literary source. It is said to have been written for the Mongol royal family. In it, there is a statement supposedly made by Genghis Khan, while he was hiding on the mountain of Burkhan Khaldun. After running away from the enemies who had raided his camp and kidnapped his wife, he is supposed to have said:

> " I have escaped with my life. I have reached Burkhan Khaldun, and I have made a shelter of elm branches. By Burkhan Khaldun, I was shielded. Every morning I shall sacrifice unto Mount Burkhan. Every day I shall pray unto it. Let the seed of my seed observe this."

Much of northern Mongolia consists of vast mountain ranges, such as the Altai and the Khentii (which includes Burkhan Khaldun, the possible burial place of Genghis Khan).

On the sacred mountain

Burkhan Khaldun mountain is about 2,662 metres (over 8,700 feet) high. The summit can only be reached from the south. To get there, you cross two swollen rivers and a wide, boggy **plateau**, before climbing steep rocky slopes.

The top of the mountain is also bare, except for an *ovoo* (shrine), consisting of a **cairn** of stones with wood wedged in it. In summer, blue scarves are tied to the shrine as symbols of the blue sky above, which is the home of the Mongolian sky spirit. Mongolians consider Burkhan Khaldun to be their most holy mountain, because of its connection with Genghis Khan.

Where should I look?

Find out more about Genghis Khan online: **www.biography.com/people/genghis-khan-9308634** or the National Geographic site **ngm.nationalgeographic.com/1996/12/genghis-khan/edwards-text**. Conn Iggulden has retold the story as a best-selling novel, called *Wolf of the Plains* (Harper, 2007). Do be aware that novelists sometimes approach the truth in a way that may benefit the excitement or drama of their book.

The first search

During the 20th century, Mongolia was ruled first by China and then by Russia. It was hard for foreigners to visit the country, and no one was allowed into the "Forbidden Zone". In 1989, some restrictions were lifted. For three years, an expedition, run jointly by Mongolian and Japanese archaeologists, combed the area around Burkhan Khaldun. It used special sound equipment to detect signs of digging. The expedition found 1,380 ancient tombs in the Burkhan Khaldun area. But work was stopped after fierce protests by local people, who regard grave sites as sacred places.

Hi-tech archaeology

What was the solution to this problem? The answer lies with modern technology, which can make a survey of the region without the need for excavating with large teams and machinery. Here are some examples:

- **Drones** fly over the site and use ground-piercing radar to show what is under the surface.

- **Satellites** circle Earth and transmit highly detailed images of the ground.

- Magnetometers (instruments that measure magnetic changes under the ground) detect the presence of metal objects.

All of these methods are being used by the Valley of the Khans Project, which was given permission to survey the Forbidden Zone in 2009. The project involves scholars and archaeologists from Mongolia as well as scientists from the University of California in the United States. The organizer, Albert Lin, says, "Using traditional archaeological methods would be disrespectful to believers. The ability to explore in a **non-invasive** way lets us try to solve this ancient secret without overstepping cultural barriers." His ultimate dream is, of course, to locate Genghis Khan's lost tomb.

You can join in!

i

The Valley of the Khans Project needs your help. Thousands of satellite images of the Burkhan Khaldun area have to be studied carefully – far too many for the team to cope with alone. You or your school are invited to lend a hand. So far, there are 100,000 volunteers. Look on the National Geographic site (**exploration. nationalgeographic.com**) and follow the instructions.

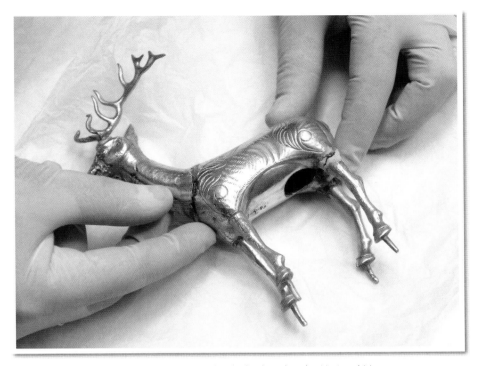

This silver deer ornamented with gold has been displayed at the National Museum in Budapest, Hungary. There are also important Genghis Khan artefacts kept by the Hermitage Museum in St Petersburg, Russia, and also many owned by the Mongolian government. Some of these formed a major exhibition which toured the world in 2007.

Research roadshow: Other "lost" sites

Genghis Khan's tomb probably exists – somewhere. Many other "lost" places have never been found, such as:

- El Dorado: El Dorado ("the Gilded One" or "the Golden One") was believed to be a South American chief who covered himself in gold dust and dived into a lake. It later came to mean an entire lost city full of gold. Many explorers, including Sir Walter Raleigh, organized expeditions to find the city but these failed.

- Avalon: Avalon ("land of apples") is the island of the dead, which features in the legends of King Arthur. The king was said to have gone there to be healed after a great battle, but he never returned. The island is thought to be in a lake in Somerset, where many apples are grown.

YOUR PARK

A city park might appear to be a tame sort of place, but it can contain links with history that come as quite a shock. In January 2013, cleaners in New York City's Central Park were hard at work. Some were restoring an 18th-century cannon, which had been on display in the park for many years. To their horror, they found inside not just a cannon ball but also an explosive charge of gunpowder. The gun had been ready to fire for over 200 years!

What is your park for?

On the surface, one park looks much like another. However, as the opening story shows, it may also contain some big surprises. Parks vary hugely, from city centre gardens to sports recreation areas, and they each have special links with the past.

To discover these links, first ask yourself what kind of park it is. Is it a formal park for strolling in, with elaborate flower gardens, water features, and statues? This kind of **urban** park was probably built in the 19th century, to make cities more attractive places in which to live and work. Or is it just a big open space, with grassy areas for picnics and sports, and a skateboard area? Most probably, your park will be somewhere in between.

Time and space

Your next task is to fix your park in its place in history as accurately as possible. This will give you a firm basis for your research. There are two elements to consider:

1. Time: When did this piece of land become a public park? There may be clues in the park itself, such as a stone commemorating the opening. And what was here before it became a park? The land has probably been used for many different things over the centuries. It would help to find old maps of the area, which show how things have changed.

2. Space: Where exactly is the park situated, and what are its boundaries? You certainly need access to maps to answer this. What district or council area is it in? Who owns the park, and who is responsible for running it? Knowing these facts will help you to focus your research more accurately.

Most parks contain links with several historical stories regarding either their origins, what they were used for, or even why they have been given the name they have. This park in Cork, Ireland, was renamed Kennedy Park in 1963 after a visit by the US President John F. Kennedy (president between 1960 and 1963). The park also contains a Victorian bandstand and 18th century cannons. Are there any parks near you which have an exciting story?

Zoom in: A potted history of parks

Long ago, most land was untouched by humans. Then, as human populations spread, more of the land was used for farming. The first parks, built about 4,000 years ago in the Middle East, were areas enclosed by walls or fences, where herds of wild animals could be hunted. These were private parks, created by rich people for their own enjoyment. The Greeks developed the first public parks in about 500 BC, where all citizens could meet, talk, and hold markets. The idea spread across Europe, and eventually to the United States. Towns grew rapidly during the 19th century, and most had specially designed new public parks. As urban populations continue to grow, and towns and cities become more hectic, these parks have become especially valued as "green" spaces for relaxing and playing games.

Using your eyes

How do you set about finding your park's links with the past? You can only do this by studying the evidence available. The best primary source is obviously the park itself. Walk through every part of the park and note down anything that puzzles or intrigues you. You could also take an old map, to help you spot changes to the layout or boundaries.

Ask yourself questions about what you see. Is the pond fed by a stream or river? If so, it may have been used as a power source once. How big and old are the trees? This can give clues to the age of the park. What are those strange lumps and bumps in the ground? They may be the buried remains of old buildings or water features. If you cannot think of an answer, put it on your list of things to research later.

Buried in the past

Some parks have a very long history, and change over time in surprising ways. The oldest public park in the United States is Boston Common in Boston, Massachusetts. Established in 1634, it has been used for many different purposes during its long history. It has seen cattle grazing, condemned prisoners being hanged, and troopers being trained. It also includes a graveyard called the Granary Burying Ground.

During the 19th century, the Gardner family, who lived next to the park, became fascinated by a tomb in the Burying Ground. The tomb began to collapse and the excited Gardners poked about in the ruins. To their horror, they unearthed a skull, still covered with golden hair. The gruesome find inspired them to research the history of the graveyard. Among other things, they discovered the skull had belonged to a girl who had died from **smallpox** a century before.

Zoom in: Using photographs

Many urban parks were laid out in the second half of the 19th century. This coincided with the development of photography, so the early history of many parks was recorded by local photographers. Their collections can often be found in local museums, or in books of local history. If you can find copies, carry them with you on your walks, and compare views today with those of a century and more ago.

The leisure time of the average person increased during the 19th century. People began to use parks more, and we can see this using photographs from the period. Cycling became very popular with both men and women at the end of the 19th century. This early photograph shows cyclists in London's Hyde Park, where bicycles were allowed from 1895.

Parks on screen

Parks also play a part in the history of cinema. Many have been used as the setting for scenes in famous films. Why do you think that parks appeal to filmmakers? Here are just a few examples:

- Regent's Park, London, features in *Harry Potter and the Philosopher's Stone* (2001), and the classic romance *Brief Encounter* (1945).

- Washington Square Park, New York, features in the sci-fi adventure *I Am Legend* (2007) and the comedy *When Harry Met Sally* (1989).

- Griffith Park, Los Angeles, features in *The Terminator* (1984) and *Back to the Future* (1985).

- Central Park, New York City, has been seen in many films, from classics such as *The Apartment* (1960) and *Annie Hall* (1977) to more modern examples, such as *Enchanted* (2007).

- Prater, Vienna, is a park which appears in many classics, including *The Third Man* (1949) and the James Bond film *The Living Daylights* (1987). Has your local park been a location for film or TV? Try looking on a website like **www.movielocationsguide.com**

New York City's Central Park has been a popular place for winter ice skating for two centuries. In the 1860s, skaters used the frozen Skating Pond. Today, an artificial ice rink is used.

Digging into documents

The other primary source of information for your research is paperwork. This includes local and national records, and contemporary articles in newspapers, books, and guidebooks. You may be able to find the original plans for the park and old maps. Aerial photographs are useful when used with maps.

Details of how and where to find these different types of evidence can be found on pages 16 to 18 of this book. You could also contact your local parks department, or park staff. They might be able to help find records showing how much workers were paid, and how many hours they worked.

Connections with the past

Stay curious about your park. Be imaginative. You could be surprised at what you find. Here are some ideas for questions to ask yourself:

- Who created the park, and why did they do it?
- What kind of activities did adults enjoy in the park?
- How has the behaviour of visitors changed throughout the park's history?
- Were there any special local events that took place here?

- Who worked in the park a century ago?

Getting the best from the internet

The internet is an astonishing source of information, but it can also be a big time-waster. Here are some ideas to help you find the evidence you want quickly and effectively:

- Look to see who produces the material. Anyone can set up a website and fill it with material. Ask what authority the writer has.
- Be precise with your search. The more specific you are, the quicker you will reach a suitable site.
- Check the date of the site (most sites show when they were last updated). A lot of information becomes out of date very quickly, as fresh research and evidence comes to light. Use sites that have been recently created or updated.
- It is easy to get distracted online, so make sure you stay focused.

A source chart

As you dig deeper in your research, a lot of facts and other material will pile up. You need a system for keeping it all in order, and making it easy to access. A source chart has three columns: one for the fact, one for the source, and one for the page or specific reference. For instance:

Topic: Sports played on Mytown Park		
INFORMATION	SOURCE	REFERENCE
First football match: Mytown FC vs Othertown Wanderers 26 October 1868	The Mytown FC Encyclopedia, Ivan Ponting (Wessex Press, 2009)	pp. 23–25
Tennis courts opened by Mayor G. Fieldhouse	Mytown Evening Chronicle	Issue Monday 6 May 1925
Skateboard park built, 1996	**www.halfpipe.com/ archivenews/96mytown**	

JERUSALEM

Jerusalem, in Israel, is one of the oldest and most famous cities in the world. Its event-packed history stretches back over 4,000 years, and it contains sites that are precious to many people throughout the world.

Why is Jerusalem so important?

Followers of three of the biggest global religions look on Jerusalem as one of the most sacred of all places. At its centre are many ancient holy sites, many of them inside the walled Old City in East Jerusalem. These are especially important for:

- Jews: Jerusalem was the place where Judaism first became a major faith, and was the Jewish religious and political centre in Biblical times. The Western Wall on Temple Mount is the last remains of the ancient Temple, and Jews still pray here.

- Christians: Jesus, the figurehead of the Christian faith, spent much time in the city, and was captured and crucified (executed on a cross) here. Christians believe the Church of the Holy **Sepulchre** stands on the site where the **crucifixion** took place.

- Muslims: The Dome of the Rock is a shrine on Temple Mount. Muslims believe this covers the place where the Prophet Muhammad (pbuh), the founder of the Islamic faith, rose up to heaven and spoke with God.

A massive subject

How do you tackle such a vast, rich, and sometimes controversial topic? Obviously, it would take a lifetime to research every aspect of Jerusalem's dramatic past. Instead, you could focus your research on one particular period of the city's history – for instance, the Roman age, or the Crusades. For a Jerusalem timeline, see page 59.

There is another problem. Jerusalem is a holy place for Jews, Christians, and Muslims. Many of the most sacred sites here, such as Temple Mount in the Old City, are strictly protected to prevent any damage. This means that excavation by archaeologists is forbidden. The result is that ancient buildings may never be found.

The Islamic shrine on Temple Mount is called the Dome of the Rock because it was built on the Foundation Stone. Jews believe this stone was the holiest part of the old Temple, and regard it as their most sacred site.

Narrow it down

i

One way of focusing your research is to draw a triangle chart. This helps you find the most convenient and simple path to your evidence. Jerusalem is a very broad topic, and the weight of information may be overwhelming. Make your job easier by narrowing it down. Identify key words that gradually lead to a smaller research area. For example:

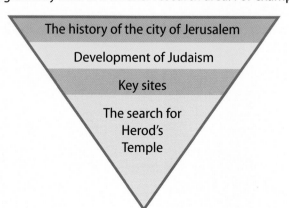

The history of the city of Jerusalem

Development of Judaism

Key sites

The search for Herod's Temple

After the two halves of Jerusalem were united in 1967, the area in front of the Western Wall was cleared to create a big open space for Jewish worshippers.

Getting Jerusalem into focus

How can you get to grips with modern Jerusalem? It is a very large urban area, covering about 126 square kilometres (49 square miles), and it is home to a population of over 960,000. One easy way to understand the place a little better would be to focus on one small area. A good area to focus on would be the ancient centre of Jerusalem, now known as the Old City. It is still ringed by high stone walls, and it contains many of the most important Jewish, Christian, and Muslim religious sites.

Inside the wall are some of the most iconic places in the world. We have already mentioned the Western Wall, the Church of the Holy Sepulchre, and the Dome of the Rock (see page 44). But other places in this small area have vital links with the past. These include the al-Aqsa **Mosque**, and the Via Dolorosa (the "Way of Suffering"), along which Jesus is thought to have carried his cross.

Research roadshow: Swimming Hezekiah's Tunnel

In 1880, teenager Jacob Eliahu swam through Hezekiah's Tunnel. This had been dug by two teams under the city during the reign of King Hezekiah about 2,500 years before, to bring in fresh water. Jacob found his way in the dark by feeling for rough chisel marks left on the tunnel walls by the ancient builders. Halfway along, he felt something different: letters. It turned out to be an inscription marking the spot where the digging teams had met – and Jacob was the first to rediscover it.

Written records

How do we find out the background to these places, many of which have been destroyed or lost? Two sources for the early centuries are the Bible and the Torah. Both the Torah and the Bible's Old Testament present a version of the beginnings of the Israeli people. They include information on the founding of Jerusalem, and on many wars and invasions. The New Testament of the Bible covers the first century of Christianity, from the life of Jesus to the spread of the faith.

Arab armies first conquered Jerusalem in AD 638, and controlled it for long periods afterwards. It has been one of the most important cities for Muslims ever since (and the al-Aqsa Mosque is mentioned in the Qur'an). Many Islamic historians recorded events in Jerusalem and Palestine, and they include evidence about crucial episodes such as the Crusades (1099–1291), which was left out by Christian and Jewish writers.

Where should I look?

Even though you may not be able to visit Jerusalem, there are many excellent sources of information online and in books. For an overview of Jerusalem's past and present through Jewish eyes, go to **www.jewishvirtuallibrary.org/jsource/Peace/jerutoc.html**. For an Islamic view, start with **islam.about.com/od/jerusalem/a/quds.htm**. For great visuals of the city, including 3D video tours of the most famous landmarks, see **jerusalem.com**. A recent full-scale history of the city is *Jerusalem: The Biography* by Simon Sebag Montefiore (Orion, 2012).

Evidence on the ground

Until the 1850s, all that was known about Jerusalem's ancient past came from books and old records. At this time, the city was ruled by the Turks, who were Muslims. But the world's most powerful nations were Christian, and included the United States, Russia, Germany, and Britain. Many people from these countries visited Jerusalem, and were thrilled to be in the birthplace of their faith.

This tiny golden bell was discovered near the Western Wall in 2011. It was probably attached to the robes of a high priest or official nearly 2,000 years ago.

Archaeologists, and others doing research, soon followed these people. In 1855, James Barclay, an American missionary, located one of the great gateways into the Old City (it is still named after him). In 1865, Charles Wilson, a British army officer, found the remains of a huge bridge from King Herod's reign (which dated from about 30 BC). In 1867, another soldier, Charles Warren, sank shafts (which means excavating a tunnel from the top down) near Temple Mount and discovered one of the main entrances to the old Temple.

Research roadshow: Roman excavators

The first archaeological dig into Jerusalem's history took place way back in AD 325. It was organized by Helena, the mother of the Roman Emperor Constantine. Being a Christian, she was very interested in discovering the tomb where Jesus was supposed to have been buried. This involved tearing down the temple built by a previous emperor and removing the earth underneath. There she claimed to have found not just the tomb, but also the cross on which Jesus had been nailed – and the nails! Later historians have doubted her claim.

Uncovering and understanding the past

This was just the beginning. In the last 150 years, hundreds of sites in Jerusalem have been uncovered and studied by archaeologists. Many of them have been restored and opened to the public, and artefacts and other historic objects have been displayed in museums to help to preserve them for future generations. Here are some of the most important places you can visit in the city:

- The Citadel: This fortress, known as the Tower of David, contains some towers that were built by King Herod. It also houses the Museum of the History of Jerusalem.

- The Burnt House: This is the basement of a house destroyed by the Romans in 70 BC when Roman soldiers sacked the city and pulled down the Temple.

- The Israel Museum: This contains many of the treasures from other excavations, including one of the oldest of all Biblical texts.

- The Mosque of Omar: This was built in 1193. This historic mosque is named after a famous Muslim ruler.

- The Ophel Archaeological Garden: Over 2,500 years of the city's history are revealed in the many layers of ruins unearthed on this site near the Temple Mount.

- The Bronfman Biblical and Archaeological Museum: This displays treasures from excavations in many areas of Jerusalem.

The world comes to Jerusalem

By the middle of the 19th century, many rulers from powerful Christian countries were visiting Jerusalem, having heard about its significance as a spiritual centre and wanting to see it for themselves.

> "Finally my triumphal entry. Crowds and dust. Tears and emotions."
>
> *Grand Duke Konstantin Nikolaevich, Russian royal family member, 1859*

> "We dismounted, and I knelt in the road and kissed the earth. Everything seemed to be just like one imagined it from one's childhood stories and the Bible."
>
> *Franz Joseph, Emperor of Austria, 1869*

A divided city

Jerusalem has grown hugely around the Old City, yet the city is still divided. Many Palestinian Arabs were angered at the creation of the Jewish homeland of Israel in 1948, which they believed took away their own homeland. This led to an invasion by neighbouring Arab states, who gained control of East Jerusalem. For nearly two decades, barbed wire and minefields divided the city. War broke out again in 1967, and the Israelis recaptured East Jerusalem.

Excavating the Old City

After the war, the Israeli government officially united the city of Jerusalem. There was a boom in excavations in the Old City. Israeli archaeologists were allowed for the first time to dig around the south end of the Western Wall and in the City of David. They have since made many amazing discoveries, including 4,000-year-old walls, Roman streets and shops, Muslim palaces, and medieval churches.

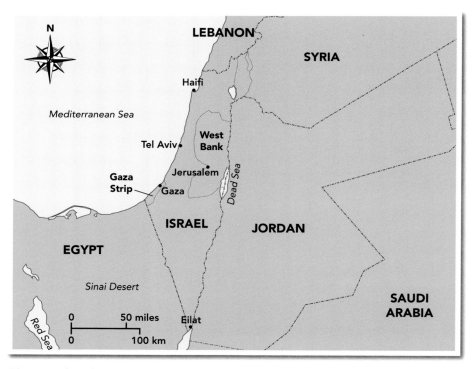

The state of Israel is surrounded by Islamic, Arabic-speaking countries, from Egypt in the south-west, through Jordan and Saudi Arabia in the east, to Syria and Lebanon to the north. Most Palestinians live in the Gaza Strip and the West Bank.

Images of the long-lost Ark of the Covenant appear on many later Jewish artefacts, such as this medieval silverware decoration for the Jewish holy text, the Torah. In the synagogue, the Torah is treated with great respect and usually is read from large scrolls. Items like this hold these scrolls.

Research roadshow: Searching for the Ark of the Covenant

Mystery still surrounds the Ark of the Covenant, the most sacred object in the old Temple. It disappeared over 2,500 years ago and has never been found. Many people have claimed to know its location (a famous fictional version plays out in the Indiana Jones film *Raiders of the Lost Ark*). In 1909, a British nobleman called Monty Parker came to Jerusalem, convinced the Ark was hidden in a tunnel south of Temple Mount. He bribed local officials, disguised himself and his team in Arab clothes, and began digging. This caused outrage, and soon Parker's men were surrounded by a mob of angry Jews and Muslims. However, nobody was killed.

BLOOD ON THE BEACH

In the summer of 2000, a team of US scientists led by Brett Phaneuf arrived on a beach on the coast of Normandy, France. They carried **echolocation** equipment, underwater vehicles with video cameras, and other machines. Using all of these, they surveyed the waters for several kilometres offshore. The result was over 120 images showing dozens of wrecked vessels strewn across the seabed. They had lain there for more than 50 years, since the invasion of Normandy in 1944 by Allied forces in World War II (1939–1945).

Landing in Normandy

The landings took place over five beaches (that the attackers named Gold, Sword, Juno, Omaha, and Utah). Above the tide line, they are characterized by banks of shingle and stretches of sand. Behind these are steep cliffs. Today, the whole area is popular with holidaymakers.

But in the early morning of 6 June 1944, the scene was horrifically different. The US Army were first to land. Dozens of landing craft, crammed with around 73,000 US soldiers, moved towards the shore. Other landing craft carried specially designed tanks that could travel through shallow water. From the cliffs, German gunners sent a blizzard of bullets and mortar shells at the approaching craft.

D-Day disaster

This was the first wave of the assault, and the place was Omaha Beach. It was part of Operation Overlord, a gigantic invasion of Normandy by Allied forces (including British, American, Canadian, and Australian troops). The task at Omaha was to cross the beach, capture the three villages behind the cliffs, then to advance south and link up with other invading units.

But the landing on Omaha Beach was a disaster. Strong winds and currents pushed the landing craft further east than planned, so most of them landed in the wrong places. Many of the craft were sunk by enemy fire. The tanks were swamped as they tried to reach the shore, and all but two of them sank in the rough waters.

D-Day landing craft got as close to shore as possible before the bow doors opened. The soldiers jumped out and struggled through the water to shore, into a blizzard of bullets and shells.

Zoom in: D-Day

Operation Overlord was the launch of an Allied invasion of Western Europe from the southern coast of Britain on 6 June 1944 (code-named "D-Day"). After weeks of heavy fighting, the Allied forces liberated France from the Nazi occupation, then advanced across Europe into Germany itself. At the same time, Soviet forces invaded Germany from the east. Overlord was the largest seaborne operation in world history, and was a decisive moment in World War II, which ended just over a year later. For more information about the Normandy invasion, see the BBC website, which has an interactive map and many other features: **www.bbc. co.uk/history/worldwars/wwtwo/launch_ani_overlord_campaign. shtml** or **www.army.mil/d-day**, the official US Army site.

The men's experience

What was it like to go into battle that day? First, the men had to stand in a landing craft, seasick and terrified. Then, they had to struggle through deep water with their heavy packs. Finally, they had to run across the beach to shelter. All this was done in the face of deadly fire from machine guns and other artillery. Here are some eyewitness accounts by US soldiers who landed in this first wave:

"The 70 pounds of equipment I was carrying sent me to the bottom. After drinking enough salt water to drown, I struggled to the surface spitting and choking. Finally making my way up to the beach, I fell down on my face and vomited what was left in my stomach."

Billy Mellander

"It was getting very crowded on the beach. Bodies of the dead and wounded kept washing up on the shore. They were coming in and out on the tide. The water turned red from all the blood."

Earl Chellis

"Our craft hit a mine that blew the front of the boat clear out of the water at the same time we were hit with 88mm shells from the beach. I found myself in the water over my head with a full pack on my back. Somehow I made it to the beach. There were bodies, body parts and blood everywhere."

Robert Watson

From the German side

How did the fighting look to the German defenders? They had laid four lines of obstacles in the water, and land mines and barbed wire on the beach. They fired on the Americans from dozens of concrete **bunkers** and **pillboxes** set on the cliffs. Here is what one young German soldier witnessed that day:

"They came at low tide. They had a long way to go up the sand and hardly any cover. They had to run all the way. Many were lying, killed or wounded. You could see when the tide rose some would move, crawling up the beach to get out of the water. At about 8 a.m. my machine gun failed and I had to use my pistol to protect myself."

Franz Gockel, 18-year-old German soldier

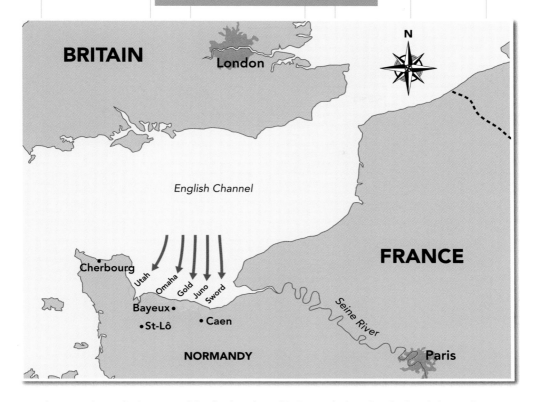

This map shows the location of the five beaches of D-Day, including Omaha Beach (second from the left).

On the 60th anniversary of the Omaha Beach landings in 2004, veterans of both sides revisited the site of the fighting. Here, German gunner Franz Gockel (left) shows a US soldier where he was positioned during the landings. You can see what Franz had to say about the day on page 54.

Seventy years later

If you visit Omaha Beach today, you can still see evidence of the events of 1944. Some of the concrete bunkers built by the Germans still stand on the cliffs. Down on the beach, historians can find fragments of shrapnel and other ammunition among the grains of sand. And at low tide, you can see the remains of a "floating harbour" (used by US troops to land equipment).

Another reminder of the battle is in the village of Colleville-sur-Mer, just behind the cliffs. This is the location of the Normandy American Cemetery, where the bodies of more than 9,000 US servicemen are buried. Most of them died during the 1944 invasion of Normandy. A memorial site, with a chapel and a statue, commemorates those whose bodies were never found.

Veterans return

Many who took part in the landings have revisited Omaha Beach since. For the 65th anniversary, on 6 June 2009, US President Barack Obama attended a major reunion at Colleville. He said, "What we must not forget is that D-Day was a time and a place where the bravery and selflessness of a few was able to change the course of an entire century".

Many of the surviving veterans are now very old and unable to travel. But large numbers of people, including veterans' relatives, history society members, and American tourists, visit the beach every year.

Research roadshow: More D-Day sites

The D-Day landings took place at many locations along the Normandy coast (and inland, where troops arrived by parachute or in gliders). Many of these sites now have cemeteries, museums, or other reminders of the 1944 invasion. Here are a few:

- The Gold Beach Museum (Musée America), Ver-sur-Mer, Normandy, covers the landings on Gold Beach.
- The Battle of Normandy Memorial Museum, Bayeux, Normandy, tells the story of the entire invasion.
- Sword Beach, Ouistreham, Normandy, was the scene of a landing by British forces.
- The Juno Beach Centre (or Normandy Canada Museum), Courseulles-sur-Mer, Normandy, chronicles the Canadian contribution to D-Day.

Several of the bunkers and some of the other concrete defences on Omaha Beach are still there and can be freely visited today. They provide a moving reminder of the events that took place in 1944, and are a stark contrast to the holidaymakers who sometimes use the beaches to sunbathe.

Where should I look?

There is a large amount of primary source material about D-Day on Omaha Beach. This comes from:

- diaries kept by officers and men
- interviews with survivors (on both sides)
- still photographs and film taken at the time
- official military records.

Many later accounts make use of these. See, for example, *Omaha Beachhead* by the Center of Military History (US Army, 1994). Yet even all this material can be interpreted in many different ways. For a study of the way the Omaha Beach story has changed over the years, look on **www.theatlantic.com/magazine/archive/1960/11/first-wave-at-omaha-beach/303365**. Or, if you can, you can always visit the beach.

TIMELINE

This timeline sets out some of the world's most famous and important sites in chronological order. There are brief descriptions of those you may not be familiar with. Places featured in the main text are marked in **bold**.

BC

c. 2 million	Great Rift Valley, East Africa (some of the earliest traces of humans have been found here)
c. 12,000	Altamira, Spain (cave used as a shelter by early humans, with miraculously preserved wall paintings)
c. 3500	**Jerusalem founded**
c. 2600	Mohenjo-Daro, Pakistan (one of the earliest permanent settlements)

AD

9	**Teutoburg Forest uprising, Germany**
79	Pompeii, Italy (Roman town engulfed (and preserved) by a volcanic eruption)
c. 1000	**Vinland, North America, is discovered**
1066	Hastings, UK (William the Conqueror's victory led to Norman rule in England)
1215	**Runnymede, UK (King John seals Magna Carta)**
c. 1220	The Silk Road (overland trade link from West to East re-established by the Mongol Empire)
1227	**Tomb of Genghis Khan, Mongolia**
1485	Bosworth Field, UK (victory for Henry VII, which began the great Tudor Age)
1520	Magellan Strait, Chile (Ferdinand Magellan was the first European to pass through this channel to reach the Pacific)
1599	Globe Theatre, London (open-air stage where many of Shakespeare's plays were first performed)
1709	Coalbrookdale, Shropshire, UK (valley settlement where advances in ironmaking kickstarted the Industrial Revolution)
1773	Boston Harbor, Massachusetts, USA (scene of the revolt called the Boston Tea Party, which helped inspire the American Revolution)
1805	Austerlitz, Czech Republic (crucial defeat of Russian and Austrian forces by the French, under Napoleon Bonaparte)
1890	**Wounded Knee, South Dakota, USA (massacre of American indians)**
1911	The South Pole, Antarctica (Amundsen's party becomes first to reach the South Pole)
1944	**Omaha Beach, France (D-Day landings, World War II)**
1945	Los Alamos, New Mexico (first atomic bomb developed and tested here)

1969	The Moon (US Apollo 11 is the first Earth mission to land on the Moon)
1989	Berlin, Germany (fall of the Berlin Wall reunites Germany)
2011	Tahrir Square, Cairo, Egypt (mass demonstrations spark the fall of President Mubarak's dictatorship during the "Arab Spring")

Timeline: Jerusalem

i

These are some of the key dates in the long history of Jerusalem.

First settlement on the site **c. 3500** — BC

— **c. 1800** City walls first built

David conquers Jerusalem **c. 1000** —

— **960** Solomon builds the first Temple

The Assyrians besiege the city, but fail to take it **701**

— **586** Jerusalem is conquered and sacked by the Babylonians

Romans capture the city **63** —

AD — **37** Herod begins to rebuild the Temple

Jesus is crucified **30** —

— **66** Jewish people revolt against Roman rule and seize control of Jerusalem

The Romans sack the city **70** and destroy the Temple

—**135** Hadrian rebuilds Jerusalem as a Roman city

The Church of the **335** Holy Sepulchre is built

— **638** Muslim Arabs conquer Jerusalem

The Dome of the Rock is built **691** —

— **1099** Christian Crusaders take control of the city

Muslims regain control **1187** — during the Third Crusade

—**1517** The Ottoman Turks begin their long rule of Jerusalem

The British capture Jerusalem **1917** — from the Turkish Empire during World War I

— **1930s** Huge increase in Jewish immigration sparks Arab riots

Creation of the state of Israel: **1948** — Jordan captures East Jerusalem

— **1967** Israel regains control of East Jerusalem

— **1980** The reunited Jerusalem becomes Israel's official capital, but the status of the city remains contentious to this day

GLOSSARY

allied describes members of a group, an alliance. This can be used to describe those fighting with the US in World War I and World War II.

archaeologist person who studies the remains of past ages

artefact tool, weapon, or other object produced by humans

atrocity cruel or savage action

authority right or power to act or command

baron lord or nobleman who is given his title by the king or queen

bunker strong shelter, often underground

cairn pile of stones built to mark a special spot or route

cavalry soldiers who fought on horseback

census survey undetaken to count a whole population, usually undertaken by the government

compensation something given to repay someone for a debt or wrong

constitution laws and principles that make up a system of government

crucifixion execution by nailing the victim to a cross

drone pilotless aircraft, controlled remotely from the ground

echolocation technique of finding or measuring an object by bouncing sound waves (echoes) off it

evidence in history, anything that helps create an accurate picture of the past

exile forced removal of a person from their native land

Germanic belonging to the peoples who lived in the area now called Germany

legion unit of the Roman army, containing between 3,000 and 6,000 troops

mosque Muslim place of worship

nomadic living the life of a nomad, someone who does not live in a permanent home, but moves around in search of food

non-invasive examining something hidden by using remote imaging rather than actually uncovering and touching it

occupy ruling of another country by an invading power

outlaw someone who is treated as a criminal, and is "outside the law"

parchment old-fashioned writing material used before modern-day paper. It is produced by stretching and flattening sheepskin.

peat soil made of rotted vegetable matter, usually found in bogs or fens

Plains Indians Native American people who lived on the Great Plains

pillbox semi-hidden military hideout, usually featuring holes in the wall through which weapons are fired

plateau high and flat area of land

primary source historical source that dates from the period itself

ravine narrow gorge or small valley

reservation area of land set aside for American Indian peoples to live on when removed from their original homes

saga Scandinavian prose story, telling of real and legendary events

satellite human-made object that orbits Earth, relaying signals and other data

scribe person whose job it was to write things down. They were used in centuries past where fewer people could read and write, so this was a skilled job.

secondary source historical source produced after the event

sepulchre vault used for housing dead bodies after burial

silt sand, clay, or similar material transported by moving or flowing water and then deposited as sediment somewhere else

smallpox dangerous infectious disease

steppe flat, dry grassy plain that covers large parts of Mongolia, as well as Siberia and southeast Europe

symbol something that represents or stands for something else (usually a material object that stands for an idea)

taboo something that is banned, forbidden, or frowned upon

tithe tax of one-tenth of a person's earnings or produce that used to be given to the church

urban belonging to a town or city

FIND OUT MORE

Books

1001 Historic Sites You Must See Before You Die, Richard Cavendish (Editor)
  (Cassell, 2008)

Battles that Changed the World (The Top Ten), Chris Oxlade
  (Franklin Watts, 2010)

Landmarks Of Britain: The Five Hundred Places That Made Our History,
  Clive Aslet (Hodder & Stoughton, 2005)

On the Map: A Mind-Expanding Exploration of the Way the World Looks, Simon
  Garfield (Gotham, 2012)

The Bumper Book of London, Becky Jones and Clare Lewis (Frances Lincoln,
  2012)

The Story of Exploration, Anna Claybourne (Usborne, 2009)

*The World Made New: Why the Age of Exploration Happened and How it Changed
  the World*, Marc Aronson (National Geographic, 2007)

Websites

www.bbc.co.uk/history/british/middle_ages/magna_01.shtml
Learn more about the Magna Carta on the BBC website.

www.historyextra.com/historic-places-to-visit
The *BBC History Magazine* website provides a selected list of historic places
to visit in the UK.

www.historyworld.net/wrldhis/plaintexthistories.asp?historyid=ab90
The History World website has a short history of the world's exploration, with
quizzes and other features.

www.hrp.org.uk
This website is an official guide to the history of the UK's royal palaces.

www.historicplaces.net
A register of many historic places in the USA and Canada, listed by state and region, or category.

www.historyteacher.net/APEuroCourse/WebLinks/WebLinks-AgeOfExploration.html
This site offers further weblinks for more on world exploration.

www.huffingtonpost.com/2011/02/25/the-most-overlooked-histo_n_827814.html#s245336&title=In_the_Shadow
A slideshow offering some information on world historic sites which are less well known.

Further research

The world is filled with places that have historical links, from battlefields and scenes of scientific discoveries to village greens and lost cities. Here are some topics you might like to explore:

- Places associated with great figures from history: Many famous people have strong links with particular locations. Maybe they were born there, or did something remarkable there. Think of author Charles Dickens walking the streets of Victorian London, or Abraham Lincoln growing up in a log cabin in Kentucky, or aviation pioneer Amelia Earhart in the central Pacific. Is there a place like this near you?

- Beautiful or dramatic places: Some landscapes have a special beauty or grandeur, which attract people through the ages. There are countless examples, such as the Lake District, the Grand Canyon, the Himalayas in Asia, and the city of Venice. Your research could include looking for paintings, photographs, and written descriptions of these places, and examining what makes them so well loved.

- Old industrial sites: Industry does not just mean huge factories. It also includes windmills, watermills (many of them very ancient), canals, and forges. There may even be connections in your neighbourhood with the history of making and transporting things. These may date back to the Middle Ages, or to the Industrial Revolution, which began in about 1700.

INDEX